Younger Me

Joshlyn Nicole

Copyright © 2022 by Joshlyn Nicole

All rights reserved.

No portion of this book may be reproduced in any form without written permission from the publisher or author, except as permitted by U.S. copyright law.

Introduction

I went to delete my old Facebook page and it asked me if I wanted to download my data first. So, I downloaded the data and as I was reading my old posts, I'm like that'll be good in a book. This book is like a published diary. It's going to show my growth from 2010 to 2016 through Facebook posts. And I give my thoughts throughout the book as well.
   Enjoy!

YOUNGER

ME

JOSHLYN

DEAR YOUNGER SELF

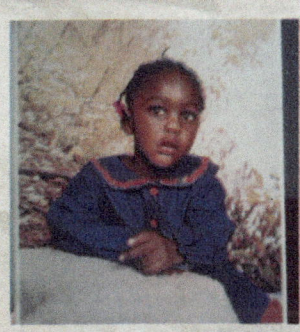

You're going to be okay.
You took on burdens
that weren't yours to carry.
You were never a failure.
You never needed to
put so much pressure
on yourself.
You have always been enough.
All of your wildest dreams will
come true.

NICOLE

A TIME WHEN IT WAS ALL SO SIMPLE

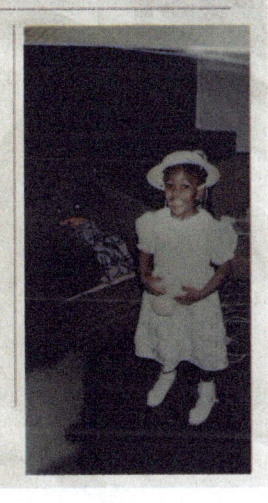

Dear Younger Self,

You're going to be okay.
You took on burdens that weren't yours to carry.
You were never a failure.
You never needed to put so much pressure on yourself.
You have always been enough.
All of your wildest dreams will come true.

Love,

Current Joshlyn Nicole

JOSHLYN

DEAR YOUNGER SELF

Enjoy every moment
Work Hard
Dream Even Bigger
Be Yourself Always

You made it through
so many tough days.
Remember shedding so many
tears.
Not sure how to push past it.

NICOLE

MEAN WORDS
WHO AM I?
HARD DAYS

These posts start in 2010. I was in the eleventh grade in high school. I started at a new school and adjusting was tough.

Remember to live your life and not the life of someone else.

Aug 19, 2010, 6:16 AM

waking up and gettin ready 4 school. hope everyone have a good day at work and school. Remember to live ur life and not the life of someone else.

Joshlyn Nicole updated her status.

Found an old picture of my agenda and I had to include it!

Believe in yourself and your dreams always. I've had dreams of being a published author forever. To see this old post of mine was wild.

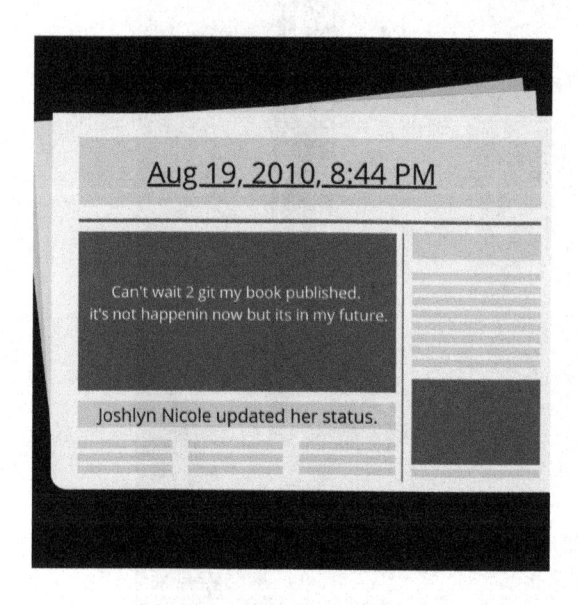

> **Aug 19, 2010, 8:44 PM**
>
> Can't wait 2 git my book published. it's not happenin now but its in my future.
>
> Joshlyn Nicole updated her status.

JOSHLYN NICOLE

DEAR YOUNGER SELF

Joshlyn Nicole updated her status. YAYYYYY!!!! im happy im getting a new fone in anotha month. a touchscreen w/ a keyboard and internet.

Aug 21, 2010, 7:05 AM

Joshlyn Nicole updated her status.

Long night ahead of me. Gotta get my hair done and lots of homework. Time for a snack. a brownie is sounding real good. LOL

Aug 22, 2010, 8:09 PM

Joshlyn Nicole updated her status

Aug 22, 2010, 10:58 AM

im thinking bout khaki skinny jeans. time to go uniform shopping again

JOSHLYN

2day i dare 2 b ME!!!

As I'm going through my posts, I'm realizing the younger me was something else.

Aug 30, 2010, 7:05 PM

i c y girls fall in luv wit playas. their game iz so smooth and swagga on point. at da end of da day u realize he dat way 2 all da girlz and ur nothing special. It doesnt hurt cuz u knew you had a playa wen ya'll got 2gotha.

Joshlyn Nicole updated her status.

Joshlyn Nicole updated her status.

Damn, do people eva stop hating. Its crazy how i tri 2 keep 2 myself but folks always wanna start something. What causes it? HAte cuz u aint me or jealousy or a little of both

Sep 3, 2010, 7:45 PM

Joshlyn Nicole updated her status.

Watching Taylor's Swift performance of You Belong With Me b4 da game brought me back 2 good times w/ 21st Century Leaders and salsa night. LOL

Sep 9, 2010, 8:06 PM

Joshlyn Nicole updated her status.

U hate because u dont like da person that looks back at u wen u look into the mirror. Sorry I cant change who I am 4 u. I can only be me and if u hate date so b it. Im not worried bout wat others say becuz dis is my life 2 live and Im gonna live life the way i want to. Low self-esteem is something in the past that i hope 2 neva look back on.
Peace And Love

September 25, 2010, 8:58 PM

Current Me: I was bullied a lot in middle and high school. I was just different from the other kids and I didn't fit in. People called me ugly, talked about my clothes, and said I smelled bad. And I remember at this time trying to understand why these kids hated me. Why did they have to be so mean to me? I used to walk with my head down because I was so afraid of what someone would say about me. So, seeing this post now makes me a little emotional. I was really fighting through it and reminding myself that it's okay to be me.

Joshlyn Nicole updated her status.

Mann, Im just so tired. Not physically but mentally. I just wanna get out of the 11th grade with honors and time is moving so slow. I have no time for da drama and bs but dats wat i deal with on a daily basis. We in high school now- grow da heck up or go bac 2 middle school. Dat is all I have to say.
Peace and Love 2 everyone.

Oct 13, 2010, 5:08 PM

Oct 16, 2010, 2:39 PM

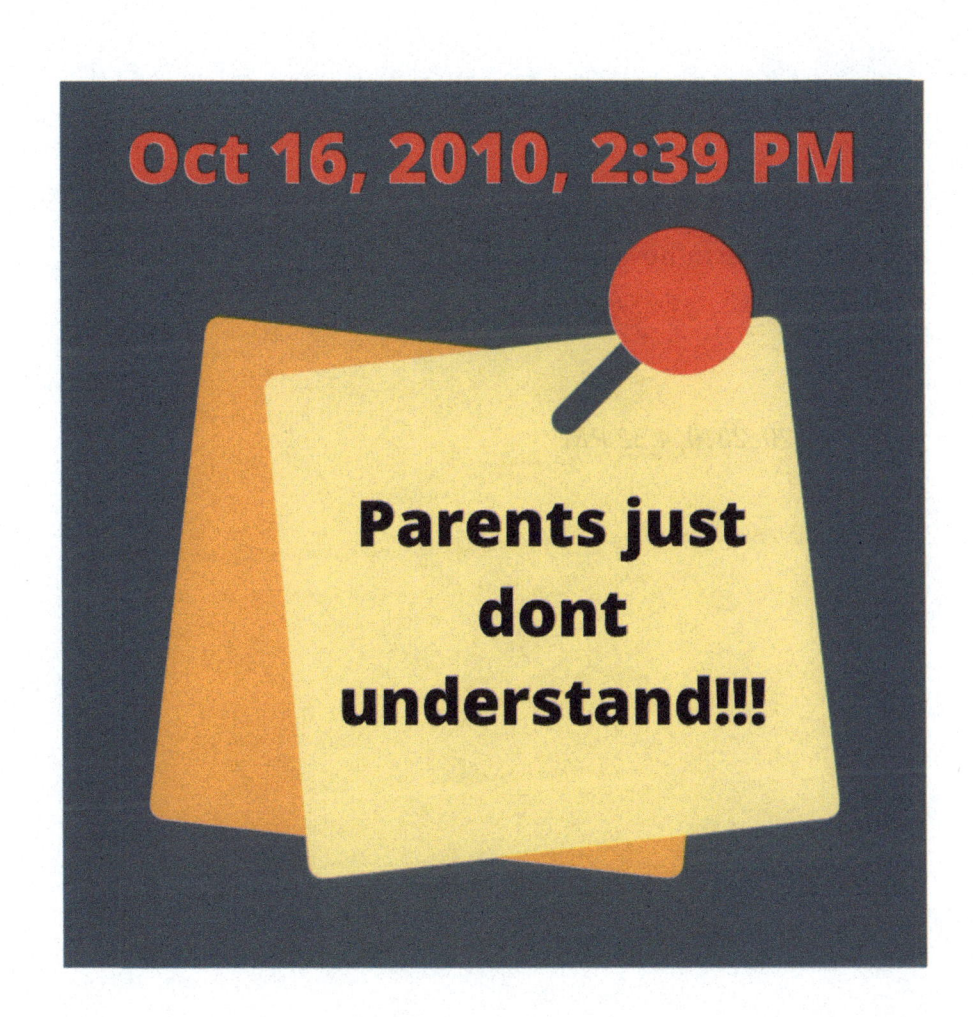

Parents just dont understand!!!

Joshlyn Nicole updated her status.

is wanderin how life is easier on sum yet harder on othas

Oct 20, 2010, 4:52 PM

‐ ‐

Joshlyn Nicole updated her status.

WHOA!! Im officially seventeen. Cnt beleve it since some years bck i wnted 2 ended thngs. Glad i didnt i wldnt have all da great friends i have. Glad god blessed me anotha year. Anyway peace nd love 2 mi associates.friends,besties, family, mi mom, mi brotha, nd da bf. 2day will b GREAT nd it is mi time 2 shine!!

Oct 30, 2010, 4:35 AM

　　Current Me: Another one that put me in my feelings. I'm still here despite it all. God has truly blessed me.

Joshlyn Nicole updated her status.

I am tired of trying 2 b liked or accepted by everyone. 2day and 4ever i DARE 2 b ME!! I hope everyone has a great day. Wait 2day is the start of spirit week. Wooh tech high titans!!

Nov 15, 2010, 6:08 AM

   Current Me: I finally realized that I'm not for everybody and that's okay. It's a great place to be in life because I'm finally comfortable in my skin and okay with being me. I really stepped out of the box and started blogs, podcasts, and channels where I openly give my opinion and just being myself. And I never thought I would do anything like that because I used to be so afraid of what people would say. Not anymore! I'm not here to impress anyone or to be liked by everyone.

Joshlyn Nicole updated her status.

Had a great night at the hockey game except no one got in a fight. Oh well maybe next game!!! LOL. Had 2 b the best night of my life!!!!!!!!

Nov 18, 2010, 6:31 AM

Joshlyn Nicole updated her status.

UMM... I have nothing interesting to post. I just hopes everyone has a GREAT day at school and work. Remember to let all the bs go, breathe in breathe out, and think happy thoughts. LOL :)

Dec 2, 2010, 6:35 AM

Joshlyn Nicole updated her status.

Midterms all this week time 4 me 2 get studying. Got 2 raise my GPA and grades. I refuse 2 fail!!

Dec 13, 2010, 6:21 PM

Joshlyn Nicole updated her status

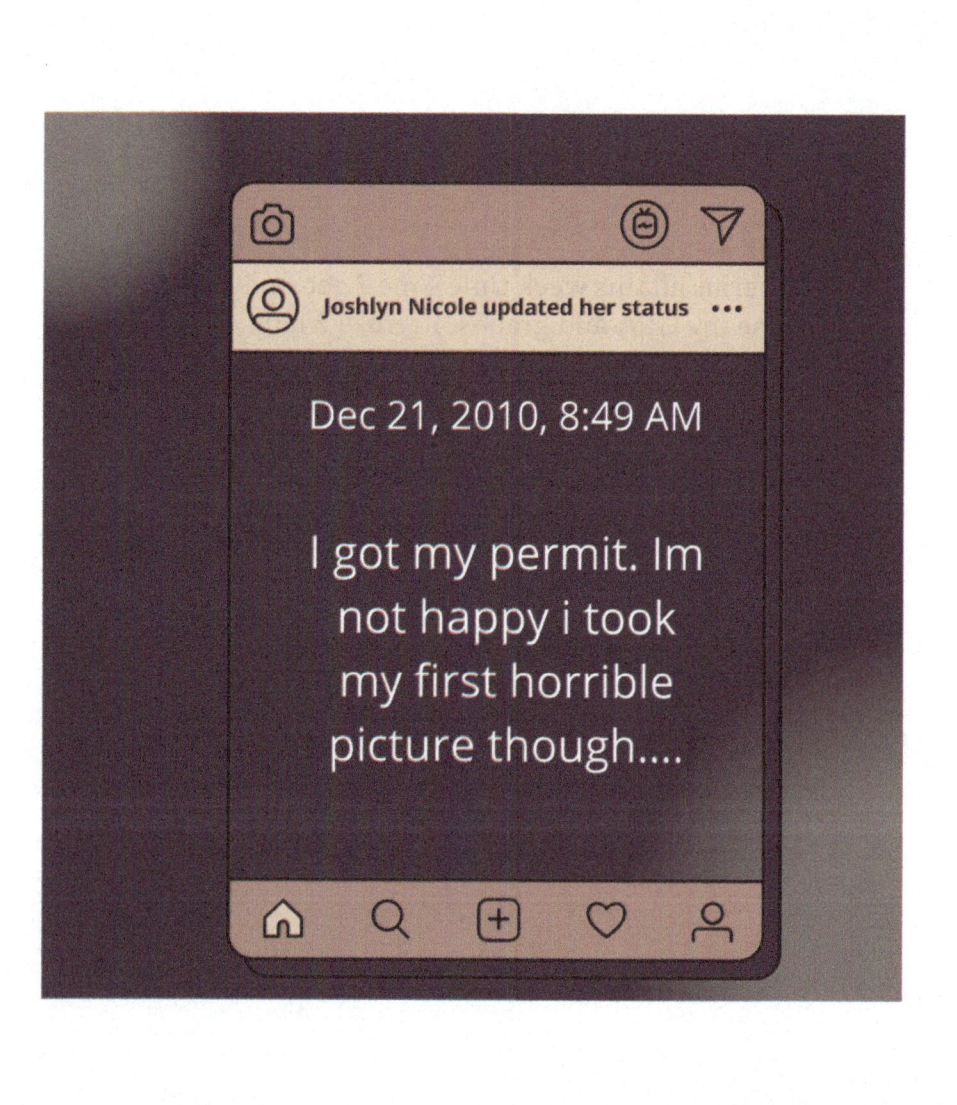

Dec 21, 2010, 8:49 AM

I got my permit. Im not happy i took my first horrible picture though....

Joshlyn Nicole updated her status.

Whoa being alone with my own thghts is scary lol. Time 2 think about happier things like food and candy!! :)

Dec 29, 2010, 2:07 PM

Joshlyn Nicole updated her status.

WHOA!! 2011 is right around the corner. No really, I can see it!!!! I am hoping for a great year and going into 2011 with a new outlook on life. It's my time to SHINE!!!

Dec 30, 2010, 9:39 AM

Joshlyn Nicole updated her status.

This year i will dare 2 me. I could care less what ppl think. It's all about ME!! lol

Jan 2, 2011, 10:31 AM

Joshlyn Nicole updated her status.

I love my mommy. Whenever im in trouble or need anything she's got my back. When it seems the world is against me my mommy is in my corner. She is so AWESOME!!

Jan 3, 2011, 5:37 PM

Joshlyn Nicole updated her status.

Thank God for waking me up this morning. Hope everyone has an AWESOME day!!

Jan 7, 2011, 6:51 AM

Joshlyn Nicole updated her status.

If i asked to change one thing in my past, it would alter my future. And quite frankly i like where i'm at!!

Jan 8, 2011, 11:55 AM

Joshlyn Nicole updated her status.

Yessssssssssssss!!! Just heard Tech High is closed 2morow. Time 2 stay up all night. Forget this math homework(for now) lol

Jan 9, 2011, 6:46 PM

Joshlyn Nicole updated her status.

Really, it wants to snow again. Im already stuck in the house...wow

Jan 11, 2011, 12:48 PM

Joshlyn Nicole updated her status.

I need the mayor of east point to get out of her pajamas and hire ppl to clean the roads. I'm tired of being stuck in the house, I'm bored, and I'm hungry. lol

Jan 13, 2011, 4:44 PM

Joshlyn Nicole updated her status.

Who wants to help me factor 5 degree polynomials? Any takers lol

Jan 17, 2011, 2:35 PM

Joshlyn Nicole updated her status.

Up eating strawberries and cream icecream even though i want french vanilla. I am also questioning and pondering life. I wander what my purpose is... SN: getting rid of all the ppl i dont need in my life :)

Jan 18, 2011, 10:15 PM

Joshlyn Nicole updated her status.

2day turned out 2 b pretty awesome! i spent the day putting things in perspective and shopping. I still got nun but love for him!

Feb 5, 2011, 6:13 PM

Joshlyn Nicole updated her status.

Time 2 work harder! stupid grades always make me super sad. i feel like i am not working up 2 my full potential....

Feb 10, 2011, 4:49 PM

YOUNGER ME

Joshlyn Nicole updated her status.

so went to homecoming at tech tonight. Wasn't my type of scene so i dipped. lol

Feb 11, 2011, 11:02 PM

Joshlyn Nicole updated her status.
Hardest part of a relationship is realizing 2 let go and move on without that person who has really became your best friend....
Apr 3, 2011, 11:29 AM

Joshlyn Nicole updated her status.

I love unlimited texting!!!!!!!

Apr 6, 2011, 10:27 AM

Joshlyn Nicole updated her status.

Haha my big bro got 2 get eight shots. almost feel bad 4 the kid but ummm not really...

Apr 6, 2011, 11:55 AM

Joshlyn Nicole updated her status.

Aha I'm single again!!!

Apr 12, 2011, 8:36 PM

Joshlyn Nicole updated her status.

I feel like I lost my best friend now that the relationship is over...

Apr 16, 2011, 9:13 PM

YOUNGER ME

Joshlyn Nicole updated her status.

From bestfriends to nothing at all. I cant even be sad about it. Just gotta move on with my life and smile big!

Apr 25, 2011, 5:46 PM

Current Me: I'm cracking up at these posts. This was my first serious "relationship" and I remember him breaking up with me over text.

Joshlyn Nicole updated her status.

I'm hearing that the NFL lockout is over. Any truth to this story?

Apr 25, 2011, 6:58 PM

Joshlyn Nicole updated her status.

YAYYYYYYYYYYYYYYYYYYYYY!!! The NFL lockout is over.

Apr 25, 2011, 7:06 PM

Joshlyn Nicole updated her status.

people dnt realize who their real friends are because they are busy trying 2 please others who really could care less about them!

May 3, 2011, 3:23 PM

Joshlyn Nicole updated her status.

Hmph...to think we could work things out was a huge mistake. You said you changed but you havent. funny how relationships also end friendships!!

May 28, 2011, 12:34 AM

Joshlyn Nicole updated her status.

Lol this dude on MARTA hiding behind his seat eating bbq chicken and im like dude i see you!

Jun 2, 2011, 2:27 PM

Joshlyn Nicole updated her status.

Hmmm a random thought for Class of 2012: we were promoted 4rm 5th grade in 2005, promoted from 8th grade in 2008 and will graduate as seniors (12th grade) in 2012!

Jun 10, 2011, 9:23 PM

Joshlyn Nicole updated her status.

Just hearing the news about Amy Winehouse. RIP Amy Winehouse

Jul 23, 2011, 2:16 PM

Joshlyn Nicole updated her status.

so the game decided to take evryone out in his new song, uncle otis. interesting lol

Jul 23, 2011, 7:24 PM

Joshlyn Nicole updated her status.

At one point or time, we have all prejudged a person without getting to know them or talked about someone behind their back. It's wrong and it's mean. I'm sorry that i am one of the people to talk about someone behind their back....

Aug 18, 2011, 7:50 PM

Joshlyn Nicole updated her status.

Falcons need to work on their defense!!

Sep 11, 2011, 1:48 PM

Joshlyn Nicole updated her status.

Execution of Troy Davis has been haulted or so they have said but no official reports have came out yet. lets hope his life have been spared once again!

Sep 21, 2011, 7:08 PM

Joshlyn Nicole updated her status.

Smh...thank you white america for teaching me that skin color still matters!

Sep 22, 2011, 5:35 AM

Joshlyn Nicole updated her status.

Today was an interesting day...lets see I protested by wearing a black shirt. I was supported because it showed I was socially aware. Long story short the silent protest was shut down and I had to put my uniform shirt back on.

Sep 22, 2011, 9:03 PM

Current Me: Around this time, I am forming my political ideas based on what's around me. As this goes on, you're going to see this change as I make sense of the world. And this is why I'm a firm believer in not holding people to their original thoughts and opinions. Allow people to grow and learn. Life is all about evolving and growing as a person.

Joshlyn Nicole updated her status.

I know there is "no place for hate" at tech high but i really hate my AP Lit class!!!

Oct 3, 2011, 7:38 AM

Joshlyn Nicole updated her status.

I have a lot on my mind and the one person I want to talk to-I can't talk to. smh people are never there for me when i need them most.

Oct 3, 2011, 9:34 PM

YOUNGER ME

Joshlyn Nicole updated her status.

Today is going to be a great day!

Oct 7, 2011, 7:08 AM

Joshlyn Nicole updated her status.

Today has been a little disappointing..

Oct 8, 2011, 7:02 PM

Joshlyn Nicole updated her status.

Only at tech high can you get suspended for standing in the hallway and get detention for uniform smh.

Oct 14, 2011, 3:40 PM

Joshlyn Nicole updated her status.

Listening to a Heavy D tribute on the radio. We need music like that now

Nov 8, 2011, 8:07 PM

Joshlyn Nicole updated her status.

I wish this drunk would stfu! and i wish I could get home! hating atlanta right now

Nov 10, 2011, 6:14 PM

Joshlyn Nicole updated her status.

I am tired of the spam on facebook. I do not want to stroll through my newsfeed and see the nasty pictures!

Nov 13, 2011, 9:17 PM

Joshlyn Nicole updated her status.

I finished reading Heart of Darkness and threw the book across the room. Oh how I hate AP Lit and stupid MLA college essays. Now it is time to write my paper...

Dec 3, 2011, 7:05 PM

Since I am broke this holiday season, all of my friends will get the gift of friendship and a few will get the gift of love!

Dec 23, 2011, 8:15 PM

Joshlyn Nicole updated her status.

Days like this I wish I never left Tri-Cities High School...Tech High was my worst mistake. So ready to graduate and get away from everyone!!

Jan 13, 2012, 5:55 PM

Joshlyn Nicole updated her status.

Picnik is closing April 19th so ive heard

Jan 22, 2012, 10:16 AM

Joshlyn Nicole updated her status.

Every adult treats me like an adorable little kid! They smile really big call me precious and sweetheart and talk to me like I'm five years old! And what do i do-smile even bigger and talk like I'm a lost little kid!

Jan 31, 2012, 4:24 PM

Current Me: I still have a baby face and it sucks! Imagine being almost 30 and nobody takes you seriously or still treats you like a kid.

Joshlyn Nicole updated her status.

BETA Club convention is officially over for me and had so much fun!!! The tests were hard, a girl's hair caught on fire and the guy put it out with her invitation to the National BETA Conference, took forever to get my room, dude fell out his seat because he was so excited, and the the talent portion was unfair. All in all a pretty good convention!!! NOW ready to graduate, pack, go away to college and never look back!

Mar 3, 2012, 9:40 PM

Joshlyn Nicole updated her status.

Just left the rally! Best experience of my life! NO JUSTICE NO PEACE!! May you rest in peace Trayvon Martin...

Mar 26, 2012, 6:27 PM

Joshlyn Nicole updated her status.

OMG!!! Just got my acceptance letter from my first-choice- Armstrong Atlantic State University!!! I am soooooooooooooooo excited!!!

Apr 4, 2012, 4:27 PM

Joshlyn Nicole updated her status.

If it wasn't for Google, I probably could not do half of my homework assignments!

Apr 8, 2012, 9:18 AM

Joshlyn Nicole updated her status.

The world is not ending, we just taking over! Class of 2012!

Apr 20, 2012, 6:10 PM

Joshlyn Nicole updated her status.

So first in the beginning of the year you stole my book bag to "teach me a lesson" and now you won't count my community service hours. Great! And on top of that, you lose thirteen of my hours and I needed you to fill out a scholarship and you didn't do it. Just great! 85 hours and you won't count them all just because they were done at Tech High. I hope this doesn't stop me from graduating with my class...

Apr 21, 2012, 7:13 AM

Current Me: There will always be people and situations in your path when you're striving for greater. Let no one or nothing stop you. Harder never means impossible.

Joshlyn Nicole updated her status.

Everything in life happens for a reason. With that being said I have no regrets in leaving Tri-Cities. I have met some amazing people at Tech and have had some great experiences. I have made some great friends and will never forget the teachers. I think I might actually be sad at graduation!

May 18, 2012, 8:41 AM

Joshlyn Nicole updated her status.

Senior year consisted of: lots of laughs, bookbag snatching, math is beautiful, senor strickland dancing whenever he had the chance to do so, a stupid science fair project, pep rallies that felt more like church than anything, friendship breakups and makeups, physics with a first time teacher, incorrect information, community service bs, amazing teachers, jr2 running for homecoming queen and lots of team work making the dream work. 2012 we made it!

May 25, 2012, 2:30 PM

Time for the next chapter of my life! I graduated high school on top of the world feeling optimistic about life. Me graduating Valedictorian is why I constantly feel like a failure. There are so many odds against Valedictorians and I'm just trying to beat the odds. The next chapter was college where my life forever changed.

JOSHLYN

Never give up on yourself.
Your dreams are still possible.

DEAR YOUNGER SELF

You're going to be okay.
You took on burdens
that weren't yours to carry.
You were never a failure.
You never needed to
put so much pressure
on yourself.
You have always been enough.
All of your wildest dreams will
come true.

NICOLE

Joshlyn Nicole updated her status.

Soooooo there is a new disease that is deadlier than AIDS. You can get this diesease from an insect known as the kissing bug. This makes me want to stay inside the house.

May 30, 2012, 10:54 AM

Joshlyn Nicole updated her status.

Convo on the phone to see if I'm eligible for a program
Lady: Are you married
Me: No
Lady: Are you pregnant?
Me: No
Lady: When is the last time you had sex?
Me: I'm not sexually active
Lady: When is the last time you had alcohol?
Me: I don't drink
Lady: I am sorry but you are not eligible for this program.

Jun 8, 2012, 5:38 PM

Current Me: I wonder what program this was. I probably qualify now. LOL

Joshlyn Nicole updated her status.

OMG!!!!! Tech High is closed. I hated that place but this makes me want to cry. Teachers are out of job and students have nowhere to go. OMG!!!!!!

Jul 3, 2012, 11:35 AM

Joshlyn Nicole updated her status.

My plan is to go to Armstrong Atlantic State University and major in healthcare administration. My goal is to maintain a 3.2 or 3.3 GPA and graduate in four years. Let's see what happens...

Jul 3, 2012, 6:31 PM

Current Me: Wow, nothing went according to plan.

Joshlyn Nicole updated her status.

Right now I am so upset! I have been such a horrible friend so I have been told. But for those that really know me you guys know the truth. If anything I have said has hurtful to anyone, I am sorry. Senior year was rough for me and I guess I did change. I never meant to act better than anyone or be such a bad friend. Never getting close to anyone again...

Jul 29, 2012, 1:12 PM

Current Me: This was the end of a friendship. Someone I had grown close to at high school. It forever changed me and I still don't like getting close to others. As I get older, I want to have close and meaningful friendships but I push people away. I don't want to ever give anybody the opportunity to hurt me. I'm working on it.

Joshlyn Nicole updated her status.

It's a new day and I'm in a better mood than yesterday. Thank you old school music for cheering me up. And when I say old school, I mean Curtis Mayfield, Marvin Gaye, Sam Cooke old school

Jul 30, 2012, 8:16 AM

Joshlyn Nicole updated her status.

Voting for the first time was interesting and funny. Funny because one of the ladies didn't believe I was 18. The story of my life lol. But anyway I'm a Georgia voter according to the sticker

Jul 31, 2012, 6:50 PM

Joshlyn Nicole updated her status.

I can appreciate honesty. But if you come at me, come at me correct. Before I was sad but now I'm just mad. You have it all wrong-I'm not a bully! I have nothing to prove to you but I do want to clear my name. Come at me bro, I'm ready!!!

Aug 3, 2012, 2:21 PM

Joshlyn Nicole updated her status.

Everybody wants change but no one is really doing anything to make it happen. One person can really make a difference. Stop putting everything on the government's shoulders!!

Aug 6, 2012, 8:16 PM

Joshlyn Nicole updated her status.

It is a great feeling when people see the good and promise in you that you don't even see. It gives you strength to keep grinding and pushing forward. I'm forever grateful for those people!

Aug 6, 2012, 9:49 PM

Joshlyn Nicole updated her status.

My last day in College "Colli" Park, Georgia until Thanksgiving of course. I'm finally all packed and ready to go.

Aug 8, 2012, 5:04 PM

Joshlyn Nicole updated her status.

Leaving Atlanta to start my new life in Savannah...

Aug 9, 2012, 11:00 AM

Joshlyn Nicole updated her status.

I made it to Savannah safely. Fixing up my dorm space. It's bigger than I expected. So far so good

Aug 10, 2012, 12:15 AM

Joshlyn Nicole updated her status.

But the good thing about today so far is I made two new friends and a cute boy smiled and said hey to me today. His smile was beautiful :)

Aug 30, 2012, 10:37 AM

Joshlyn Nicole updated her status.

I want to be a published author. Just finished typing my second novel of many. Feeling accomplished right now

Sep 2, 2012, 9:48 AM

Joshlyn Nicole updated her status.

Oh yeah I got summoned for jury duty in Atlanta. Problem is I live in Savannah. Let's hope I will be able to straighten this out and not get arrested for contempt of court.

Sep 10, 2012, 12:16 AM

Joshlyn Nicole updated her status.

I know exactly where I was on 9/11/2001. I was in the cafeteria and they (not sure who) brought in the television so we could see what happened. The teachers were really upset and students were leaving left and right. Yep, I remember that day

Sep 11, 2012, 3:01 PM

Joshlyn Nicole updated her status.

My English professor: Well, I'm going to let you guys go early...because it's Tuesday.
Keep in mind that this is an eight o'clock English class. Best news all day!!!

Sep 18, 2012, 8:52 AM

Joshlyn Nicole updated her status.

People know crazy when they see it. They are just waiting for you to do or say something that will confirm it....

Sep 20, 2012, 1:11 AM

Joshlyn Nicole updated her status.

I went to the dining hall and I swear everyday the food gets worst and worst. So now I'm in my room eating cheddar jalapeno cheetos, chicken flavored noodles, salt and vinegar chips and a banana nut muffin.

Sep 20, 2012, 8:14 PM

Joshlyn Nicole updated her status.

I have been through so much that I can't help but smile. :) I'm just lucky to be where I am today and that the things I've been through didn't stop me from getting here...

Sep 25, 2012, 12:21 AM

Joshlyn Nicole updated her status.

Today was a good day--in the words of Ice Cube! Drinking tea and studying notes for art appreciation. Going to bed early. Never getting an 8 am class again-Lesson Learned!!

Oct 3, 2012, 10:59 PM

Joshlyn Nicole updated her status.

I'm glad I didn't drop art appreciation because of one bad test. I studied hard and paid more attention in class which made today's test seem so easy. I learned life can either make you or break you. You can either quit or keep living! Life made me and is the reason I keep on keeping on!

Oct 4, 2012, 10:54 AM

Joshlyn Nicole updated her status.

It seems everyone was telling me to drop this art appreciation class because I didn't do well on the first exam. But I told them I would work hard and ace the next test. On my first exam, I got a 36 and on my second exam I got a 98. Studying and hard work are the keys to being successful in college. LESSON LEARNED!

Oct 11, 2012, 11:00 AM

Joshlyn Nicole updated her status.

I've been down so long that it feels so good to be soooo relaxed and listening to music! My friends will never understand what I have been through the first two months of college because I couldn't tell them, I spent many nights in my room crying my eyes out. Today is a new day and I kept my head up which is why I smile. I came to terms that I would not have to do what everyone else is doing to fit in. I FEEL SO MUCH BETTER!! :)

Oct 25, 2012, 2:30 PM

   Current Me: I was struggling in college because I felt out of place and just had a hard time adjusting.

Joshlyn Nicole updated her status.

I have always prided myself on being different and not doing what others are doing to fit in. In college, that seems to be my downfall. What do you do when you just don't fit? Do you try to fit in or continue being yourself? I have never felt so alone before college-I just want to pack up and go home...

Nov 3, 2012, 3:51 PM

Joshlyn Nicole updated her status.

I put zero effort into my first semester of college and my grades are evidence of that. I played around and I turnt up way too much. I look back and see the errors in my ways. I'll study harder and focus more next semester. Here I am in jeopardy of losing my scholarship and I'm maxed out on loans. Gots to do better. 2 A's, 1 B and 2 C's=final grades for the semester

Dec 13, 2012, 2:53 PM

Joshlyn Nicole updated her status.

We got our wake up call and retiring the phrases "379 turn up" and "chuck it as a lose". 379 go study!

We got next semester as long as we motivate one another to do what we have to do!

Dec 14, 2012, 2:00 PM

Current Me: Yeah, it all came crashing down.

Joshlyn Nicole updated her status.

I've learned not to push people away because not everyone will walk out of my life. Not everyone in this world is out to hurt us. Your best friends are really made in college! Lessons Learned...

Dec 19, 2012, 8:38 PM

Joshlyn Nicole updated her status.

I have a tendency to completly cut people out of my life when I'm upset with them. I don't know if that's a bad thing or not

Dec 20, 2012, 8:40 PM

Joshlyn Nicole updated her status.

Taylor is like my bestest friend and my sista from anotha motha!! We been through so much ish together and I'm glad we're still friends. She's sooooo prettyful and I love her!!

Dec 31, 2012, 10:43 PM

Dec 31, 2012, 10:57 PM

God gives the hardest battles to his strongest soldiers! Keep ya head up and stay strong. He'll make a way out of no way. I'm a living testimony of this.

Joshlyn Nicole updated her status.

Joshlyn Nicole updated her status.

I'm using a 1-subject notebook for four subjects. Let's see how this works out!

Jan 7, 2013, 1:26 PM

Joshlyn Nicole updated her status.

I'm a failure at life and there's not a redo button to push. In time, I shall get over this.

Jan 9, 2013, 8:58 PM

Joshlyn Nicole updated her status.

If I told people my biggest secret, I wonder how they

would react. Would they treat me differently? I know they would see me differently. Nothing to do but keep it hidden...

Jan 14, 2013, 11:26 AM

Joshlyn Nicole updated her status.

I'm soooooo *cough* *cough* sick and I have no one to take care of me! Guess I'll just lay in bed and listen to Lonely by Akon

Jan 18, 2013, 8:43 AM

Joshlyn Nicole updated her status.

Wtf! There was a police car chase, a loose convict on campus and we had a fire alarm at 3 am because someone wants to set the bulletin board on fire. And now I can't sleep

Jan 21, 2013, 4:48 AM

Joshlyn Nicole updated her status.

Today is one of those days where I wish someone anybody understood what I was going through and what's it like to be in my position. I just want to be happy. I'm tired of feeling like a screw-up every minute. But how can I be happy when a mistake has turned into a lifelong lesson?

Jan 28, 2013, 3:49 PM

Joshlyn Nicole updated her status.

That great moment when you don't want to go to class and you find out it is cancelled! :)...I am done for the day and it is time for a well-needed nap! Today is going great!!!

Feb 26, 2013, 12:30 PM

Cat's out the bag now! 15 weeks and healthy

Mar 19, 2013, 5:33 PM

Current Me: I was 19 and pregnant and in college. Probably one of the toughest moments in my life. I had to hide this pregnancy just to finish the year off strong. There was so much drama surrounding my first pregnancy and though I'm smiling, it was the most depressing time of my life.

Joshlyn Nicole updated her status.

I'm going to be having a little boy...found out yesterday!!!! He's such an active little boy already. I'm halfway there and we're excited!!

Apr 16, 2013, 2:11 PM

Joshlyn Nicole updated her status.

I really hate school but I don't have any other plans. I really want a summer job but job hunting is not easy. I feel so lost when it seems everyone else has it together...

Apr 17, 2013, 4:49 PM

Joshlyn Nicole updated her status.

I will always remember us riding by that funeral with RIP by Jezzy blasting out the car speakers. We didn't know whether to laugh or to be embarrassed...that was the highlight of the day yesterday! Have a great Sunday folks!!

Apr 28, 2013, 11:09 AM

I think by this point I've gotten through the semester. I finished my first year of college and headed back home to figure out my life. And boy the journey was just starting.

YOUNGER ME

Joshlyn Nicole is feeling helpless.

My mom finally admitted that she doesn't like the person I chose for myself. It hurts but what can I do? It makes me upset that she doesn't want us together and doing everything to break us up. She says he doesn't care or love me but he has proved to me otherwise. I found true happiness but she's not happy for me. She even told me he's the worst guy I could have picked. I just want to leave and never come back

May 12, 2013, 5:36 PM

Current Me: Looking back on posts during this time just makes me incredibly sad. There was just so much going on and I was still trying to figure out my life. I mean even today, I'm trying to figure it out. And seeing this post made me realize what the problem really is in my life. I need to be on my own and find happiness again.

Joshlyn Nicole updated her status.

I think today was the defining moment of me and my mom's relationship. I can't put it into words but I think she's come full circle with the pregnancy. Now she's making me fish and grits for dinner!!

May 18, 2013, 8:29 PM

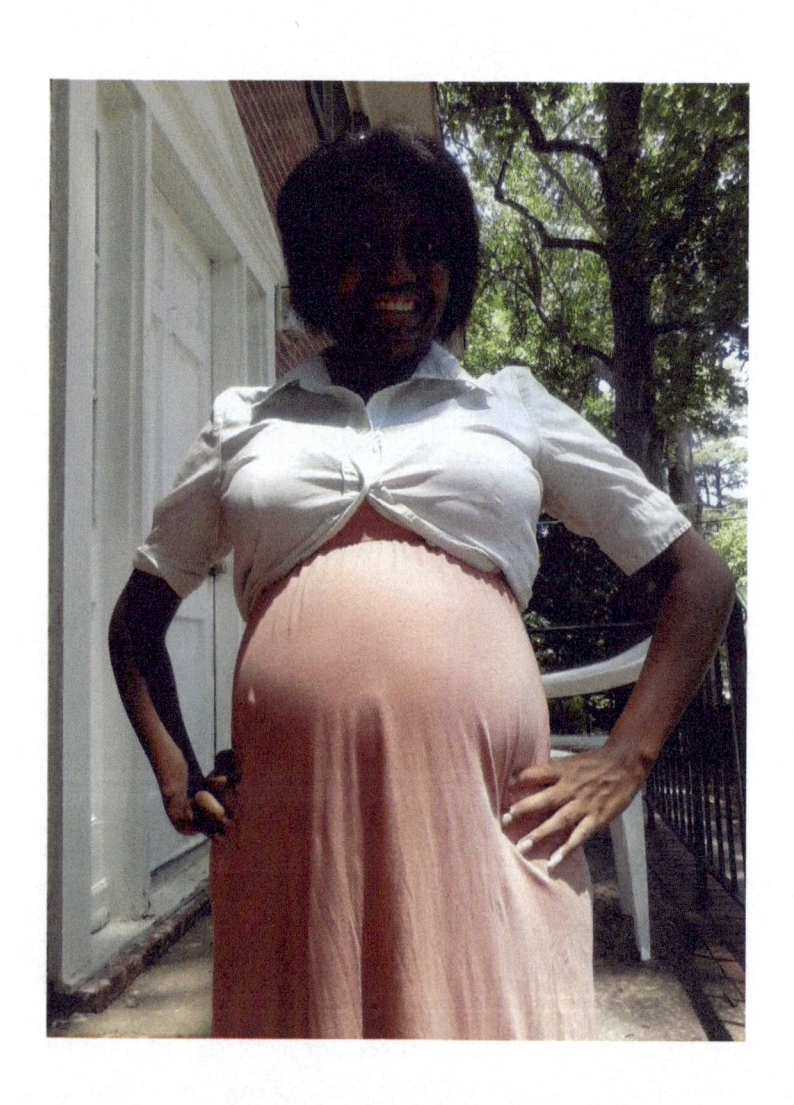

Today was very eventful. Had an interview and offered a position. The best part is the pay is great and I can work from home. And also started the first step of transferring to Atlanta Metro...just have to get my paperwork in. The best thing about today is all the compliments about how beautiful I am and how young I look even though this one chick thought I was 13 haha. Week 28 is looking great so far and this sweet potato pie is a slice of Heaven right now!

Jun 14, 2013, 4:13 PM

Joshlyn Nicole updated her status.

It's time for me to live my own life. Like I can't do this anymore. Always wanting approval and worried about what others think. I never put my happiness first. This is a lose-lose situation. So it's time for me to live my own life, make my own decisions and be happy.

Aug 22, 2013, 12:30 PM

Joshlyn Nicole updated her status.

I think Raylan needs anger management for babies if that even exists. He can go from 0 to a 20 in no time flat. He doesn't like his rocker, he doesn't like his swing, he doesn't like his crib, he doesn't like any of his toys and he doesn't like the activity mat. And on top of that he wants to eat almost every hour. I'm frustrated and don't know what to do anymore when he cries...besides cry with him. Is this normal?

Sep 13, 2013, 1:41 PM

Joshlyn Nicole updated her status.

Worked a 9 hour shift at Macy's. My first real day on the job would be Black Friday. Lol it was crazy but fun. I am tired and just want to go to bed...

Nov 29, 2013, 10:44 PM

Dec 6, 2013, 6:27 PM

I wish things were better and I wish I was happier...

Joshlyn Nicole updated her status.

Joshlyn Nicole updated her status.

Spit up on my shirt is now like a necklace dressing up a plain shirt...

Dec 7, 2013, 7:00 PM

Joshlyn Nicole updated her status.

It's a lot of people I'm glad I'm not friends with and it's a lot people I'm glad I've grown closer too. You can't take everyone down the road with you and not everyone wants to see you happy. Glad I've grown enough to see that and glad I'm grown enough for it not to faze me as much as it once did.

Dec 9, 2013, 5:40 PM

Joshlyn Nicole updated her status.

For the first time in months, I am truly happy. I'm putting those dark days behind me and moving forward.

Dec 19, 2013, 10:19 PM

Current Me: I slipped into darkness a few times after this. I'm just learning how to stay positive through it all and know that there will always be light. My life has been one rollercoaster, to say the least.

Joshlyn Nicole updated her status.

I tend to overthink instead of living in the moment. I tend to make others happy but make myself unhappy. When will I take control over my own life and do what makes me happy be with who makes me happy and forget what others think...

Dec 20, 2013, 7:13 PM

Joshlyn Nicole updated her status. *Dec 26, 2013, 6:52 PM*

What makes us perfect are our imperfections.

Joshlyn Nicole updated her status.

Be a light, you never know when someone is surrounded by darkness.

Dec 31, 2013, 1:49 PM

Joshlyn Nicole updated her status.

First time dropping Raylan off at school and I'm a nervous wreck. I don't know how I'm going to focus on school today.

Jan 27, 2014, 7:33 AM

Joshlyn Nicole updated her status.

Just have to do what I feel is right and take a step out on my own. I need a change in my life.

Feb 4, 2014, 2:59 PM

Joshlyn Nicole updated her status.

I always overthink and create imaginary problems. I just need to believe and be happy in the decisions I make.

Feb 5, 2014, 9:19 PM

Joshlyn Nicole updated her status.

I realized today that I can't just zone in on the negative when there's so many things to be blessed about. Shoot, I'm alive and someone else can't say that. I realized that His plan is bigger than my plan is for myself. I have to be patient and take it day by day. I don't have a job but I love the time I can spend with my son and the time I get to focus on school. So I'm just going to wait on that right job opportunity and keep filling out these job applications. There is nothing wrong with feeling weak or tired, the problem is when we actually give up.

Feb 25, 2014, 6:36 PM

The government pins the middle class and the lower class against each other to get the attention off their dirt. And they're laughing while y'all fighting over crumbs.

Mar 3, 2014, 6:26 PM

Joshlyn Nicole updated her status.

All this pi talk makes me want pie

Mar 14, 2014, 3:15 PM

Joshlyn Nicole updated her status.

Sometimes I feel like giving up and like there's no way to go on but I get up everyday and push forward.

Mar 18, 2014, 9:24 PM

Joshlyn Nicole updated her status.

I just wish something would come through for me...

Mar 19, 2014, 10:44 AM

Joshlyn Nicole updated her status.

I can act like it's all good but I really feel broken, alone and just hurt.

Mar 26, 2014, 11:27 PM

Joshlyn Nicole is feeling blessed.

Everything is going to slowly fall into place when they're supposed to fall into place. No rush. No worries. Everything I want is still going to happen.

Apr 8, 2014, 5:45 PM

Joshlyn Nicole updated her status.

My dreams seem to be in reach but I can't reach them.

May 30, 2014, 3:07 AM

Joshlyn Nicole is feeling confused.

Apart of me knows it is over and I should just give up and move on. But the other part is still hopeful. Which part of me is right?

Jun 13, 2014, 8:01 PM

Joshlyn Nicole updated her status.

I realized I don't like to hang out anymore. I barely respond to messages and calls. I just rather be alone and have no friends. Lol and it's not as bad as it sounds.

Jun 29, 2014, 11:06 AM

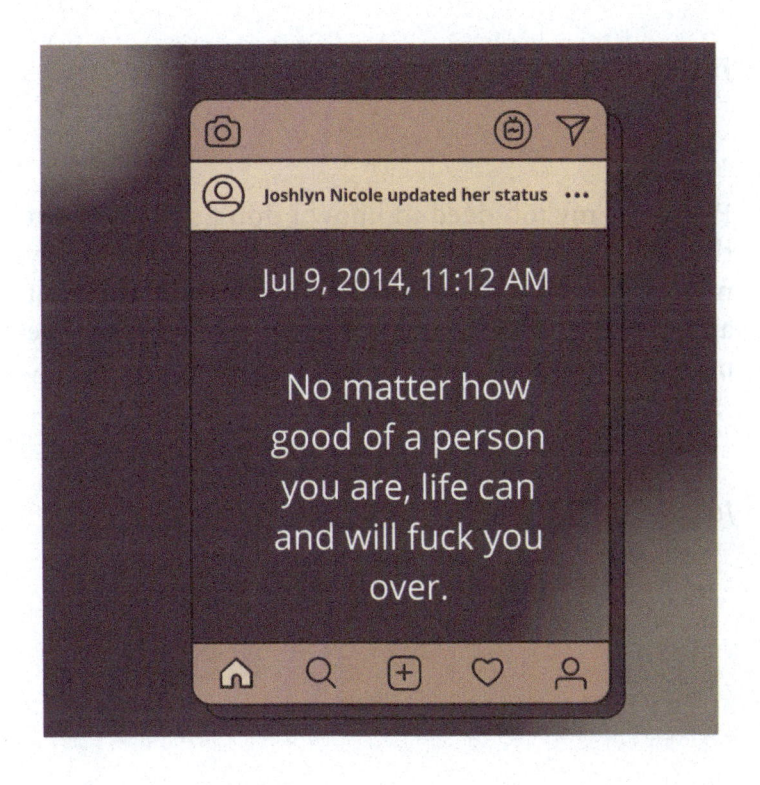

Joshlyn Nicole updated her status

Jul 9, 2014, 11:12 AM

No matter how good of a person you are, life can and will fuck you over.

Joshlyn Nicole updated her status.

People at my job need to know I don't give af about this job so trying to run and tell to throw dirt on my name is really a waste of time. I'm on my way out anyway so go ahead and speed up the process. I've never met so many messy grown folks in my life.

Jul 28, 2014, 12:04 PM

Joshlyn Nicole updated her status.

My whole life is just an EPIC fail. Like I'm just a complete failure. I just suck at this whole life thing. Nothing ever goes right for me.

Aug 15, 2014, 12:04 PM

Joshlyn Nicole updated her status.

How do I change the world so I can make a better tomorrow for my son?

Aug 24, 2014, 11:10 PM

Joshlyn Nicole is feeling blessed.

So little did I know that I had someone advocating for me at Year Up and really wanted me to succeed and be in the program. And the one person I thought was on my team at Year Up was calling me unprofessional and telling others that I needed anger management. The moral of the story is some people are for you and others aren't. Be thankful for those in your corner. Because she advocated for me and felt she had a connection to me, I got back in Year Up and she's my new case manager.

Sep 3, 2014, 1:47 PM

Joshlyn Nicole updated her status.

Just have to remember God has a bigger plan for me than I have for myself. I just have to keep pushing forward no matter how hard it gets.

Sep 29, 2014, 6:39 AM

Joshlyn Nicole updated her status.

When I think there is no possible way to go on, I just think how far I've already come. I just wish I could see into the future and know all the hard work will pay off in the end.

Jan 4, 2015, 8:46 PM

Joshlyn Nicole updated her status.

My college dorm room number was 184 and Raylan was born on 8/14. Everything in life happens for a reason.

Jan 7, 2015, 7:54 PM

The Year Up journey was not an easy journey but I made it. I overcame all the struggles and came out on top. A lot of people doubted me to make it this far and even graduate because they felt I had too many obstacles in my way. Because of this journey, I know the true definition of strength and that I can do anything as long as I stay determined. I wanted to give up on myself and this program because things got really tough in this program but I fought through it all. I've made amazing friends, gained skills to become Corporate America ready, skills that personally and professionally developed me into the person I am today and showed me that hard work truly pays off. The beginning of a journey is usually rocky, the middle is cloudy and you're not sure whether to turn back or keep moving forward and the ending is usually beautiful.

Jul 28, 2015, 7:04 AM

Current Me: This was a pivotal moment for me. I went through a lot to get through this program and I overcame it. This program changed me in so many ways.

Joshlyn Nicole updated her status.

It's okay not to be okay sometimes. Just as long as you don't stay in that place. Get back up, keep it moving and never give up. You haven't failed until you stopped trying. Starting over once again and that's okay too. I'll get where I'm trying to go just not as fast as I had hoped.

Sep 1, 2015, 8:16 PM

Never a victim, always a survivor. Life can throw all types of things at me and I'll overcome everytime.

Sep 17, 2015, 4:04 PM

Joshlyn Nicole updated her status.

First interview of the year and I'm a nervous wreck. I'm not nervous about the interview, I'm just tired of the whole interviewing process. I had 7 interviews in 2015 with no luck whatsoever. And the interviewers liked me but I wasn't the right fit particularly because of age and lack of work experience. I'm trying to remain optimistic about this opportunity but I'm just feeling like I'll never be good enough for any of these companies. And what sucks is the jobs I used to get before I obtained my Associates' Degrees, I am now overqualified. I just don't know about this.

Jan 8, 2016, 8:41 AM

Current Me: Funny enough, I'm going through this again as I try to reenter the workforce. Reading through my feed, I'm realizing I always had an issue with getting a job. I could never find the right opportunity. It either didn't pay enough, didn't work with my schedule or I couldn't find childcare. I pray one day the right opportunity comes along and gets better for me.

Joshlyn Nicole updated her status.

I didn't win Powerball but my company just released my W-2's online. A win is a win. Lol..

Jan 14, 2016, 12:07 AM

Joshlyn Nicole updated her status.

When you order a pizza online and literally stalk your pizza's life. Watching it go from the baking stage to the quality check stage and then the delivery stage. Come on pizza, you're almost there!

Jan 21, 2016, 7:51 PM

I wrote my first resignation letter ever and it was a pain. This is my first time quitting properly and being able to leave a company with the ability to return and get a reference from a manager. Today is my last day at this desk, on the phone and in this chair. It's kind of bittersweet but I know where I'm headed is far better than being stuck and complacent in a job that was leading nowhere fast. My advice to anyone is to find your passion, never get complacent and trust the journey.

Jan 22, 2016, 8:37 AM

   Current Me: I decided to take a break from college to figure out what I wanted to do in life. And because my job was a co-op, I could no longer work the job. Like I said, I've been through it trying to find stable employment. I'm having an even harder time now.

Joshlyn Nicole updated her status.

I work hard for everything I have in my life so no one can ever say out their mouth that they made me or that I'm where I am because of them.

Feb 29, 2016, 3:05 PM

So I took a bunch of political quizzes to determine if I'm a Democrat or Republican and to see how my views align with those of the party. I took a total of ten quizzes from different sources from PBS, PewResearch and Teen Vogue. Out of the ten, I got Democrat once. I was either getting Republican or Independent. And I was more conservative and moderate than liberal. I'm just confused with life right now. I'll be voting Independent in November.

Jul 10, 2016, 10:20 AM

    Current Me: This was a time in my life when my mindset was changing and I was questioning things I was taught my entire life. This is also around the time I left the Democrat party and became an Independent voter. Best decision I made in my life.

Joshlyn Nicole updated her status.

When you go against the grain, some people want to isolate you or make you think like them. You're allowed to think how you want to think and to have your own opinions. I love seeing different opinions because it gives perspective on things. But lately, I keep seeing the same rhetoric and I'm like where are the people that are going against the grain and letting their opinions be known even if it's unpopular? We're all spitting opinions at the end of the day so why get mad or try to argue with someone else's opinion.

Jul 11, 2016, 7:46 PM

Current Me: And this is when I started losing friends because of my thoughts. I just decided to create a new page because it got to be a bit much.

Joshlyn Nicole updated her status.

The media wants a race war and the system wants us divided. Looks like it's working.

Jul 12, 2016, 8:47 PM

Joshlyn Nicole updated her status.

I don't know what the solution is but what we don't need is a race war. Be careful who you get your information from. Do your own research. Form your own opinions. Some of these facts that are floating around are just opinions and generalizations. Be aware of folks telling you to stay woke but still asleep their damn selves. Just be safe out here folks!

Be rational and think through everything. Make sure everything you do is with a purpose. Live your life to the fullest. Don't be afraid to continue to live your life. Be aware of who you are and what that means.

Continue to change the world so one day there are no color lines and we can all be viewed as humans and not by the color of our skin.

Jul 13, 2016, 7:19 PM

Joshlyn Nicole updated her status.

Being divided is not going to bring about solutions or change. It's important to stand as one during this time where the system and the media wants to divide us.

Jul 13, 2016, 11:08 PM

Joshlyn Nicole updated her status.

If you don't think change begins in our own communities then you're delusional as hell.

Jul 14, 2016, 4:06 PM

Joshlyn Nicole updated her status.

Your right now doesn't have to be your forever. Dust yourself off and try again...

Jul 15, 2016, 8:03 PM

Joshlyn Nicole updated her status.

Rent keeps going up but wages are staying the same. Watching this program and just stated that a person would have to work 72 hours at 7.25 to afford a 1 bedroom downtown Atlanta and 90 hours for a 2 bedroom.

Jul 24, 2016, 11:24 AM

Current Me: Foreshadowing the current housing crisis...

Joshlyn Nicole updated her status.

Just because you're a faithful church goer doesn't mean you're not a sinner. Please don't judge me on how I choose to worship my God because you worship differently than me. Sometimes the devil is in the pulpit preaching the good word.

Aug 5, 2016, 4:25 PM

Joshlyn Nicole updated her status.

You grow up believing that you can live the "American Dream" but they never told you that because of your skin color your American dream is different than your white counterparts. They never told you you would have to work twice as hard and be twice as good just to be equal. They never told you how valuable your life was because they knew if you knew you would be more powerful than them. They made you believe that the person that looked like you was your competition and not your brother or sister. They convinced you your life didn't matter by putting drugs and guns in the communities and they watched that same community fall apart and self-destruct.

They convinced you that you were a victim and you use that as an excuse not to get ahead. They never taught you about money, investment and wealth because they don't want you to win and they never want you to be equal to them. They told you to create your own culture and fit but then deem that culture as unprofessional, unkempt and ghetto while they can coin it as trendy. But who are they and who are you?

Aug 12, 2016, 2:37 PM

Joshlyn Nicole updated her status.

Even if I don't like you or we went our separate ways, I still wish you the best. I don't have it in me to pray for your downfall. I want us all to make it.

Aug 27, 2016, 1:28 PM

Joshlyn Nicole updated her status.

Everyone is repeating the same thoughts for the same topic. Are people thinking for themselves or reading from some bs script? I like to see opposing opinions and healthy debates but that's lacking lately. I'm honestly bored and disappointed. I like seeing things from different perspectives and being stimulated by great conversation. I like facts, I like to know why and I like to be educated without being belittled.

Aug 28, 2016, 10:15 PM

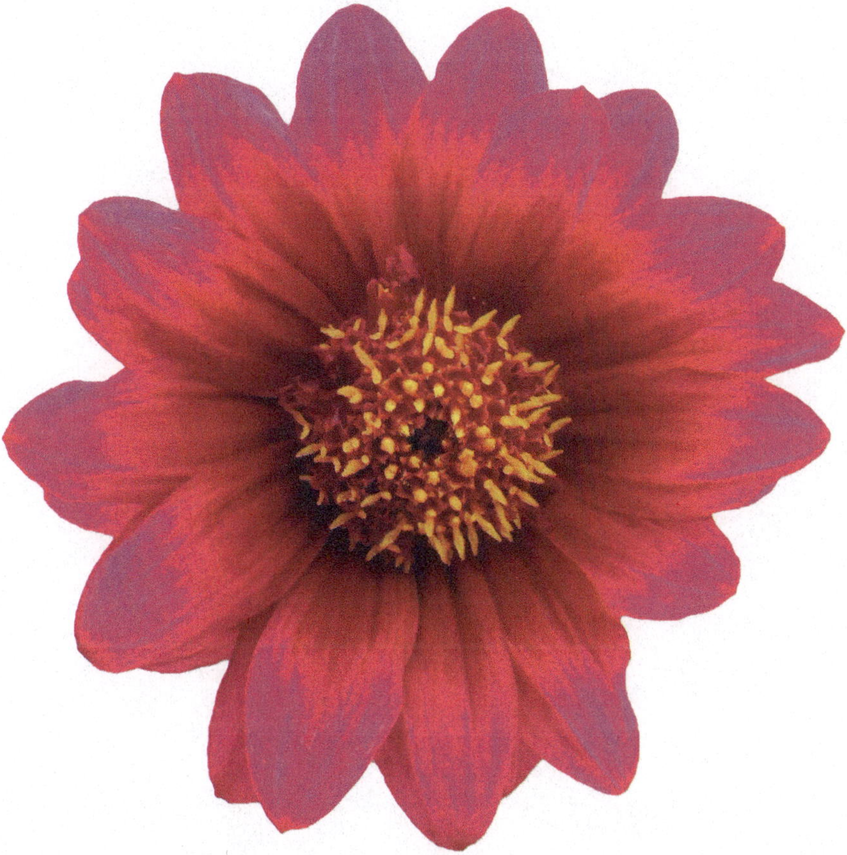

Joshlyn Nicole updated her status.

My dream since I was 7 was to be a published author. I owe it to myself to get this done. I don't know how but I'll figure it out. Feels good to get back to writing. I was afraid start this blog but I know it'll give me the motivation and momentum I need to accomplish my dream of being a published author.

Sep 30, 2016, 1:09 PM

Joshlyn Nicole updated her status.

If each person could work on being a decent human being, the world would be a better place. If we could each give more than we take, the world would be a much better place. If we could see each other as brothers and sisters no matter what race or background, the world would be a better place. If we loved and not spewed hate, the world would be a much better place.

Oct 2, 2016, 7:26 PM

Joshlyn Nicole updated her status.

Welfare is not meant to help you; it's meant to trap you and keep you dependent on the system. Do away with welfare and replace with better wages, training programs for skills and job growth. That way people can afford to live without it. But until then, don't even think about doing away with welfare.

Oct 14, 2016, 1:37 PM

Joshlyn Nicole updated her status.

No, I don't have everything in life. I just make the best out of what I do have in life. Whether I'm up or I'm down, God continues blessing me. No matter what I'm going through in life, I know I can get through it. Feeling motivated more than ever now.

Oct 29, 2016, 9:05 PM

■--■

Joshlyn Nicole updated her status.

I'm ready to get to that point in life where my money begins to work for me.

Nov 17, 2016, 2:45 PM

Joshlyn Nicole updated her status.

There are so many victims on my timeline...it's sickening. The world doesn't owe you shit.

Nov 30, 2016, 1:22 PM

Joshlyn Nicole updated her status.

Strippers are winning. Meanwhile I'm going to school getting in debt and working full-time and I can't even make it drizzle. What is life?

Dec 9, 2016, 4:11 PM

Joshlyn Nicole updated her status.

I'm not here to impress or stunt on others. I'm just trying to be better than I was yesterday. My journey is uniquely mine and I'm on my own path. Stop focusing on everyone else's journey and focus on your own journey. No time to hate or be jealous. Just get where you're trying to go.

Dec 11, 2016, 7:13 PM

Joshlyn Nicole updated her status.

3 and 4 times the rent just to get a place....This honest living ain't cutting it.

Dec 13, 2016, 11:42 AM

Joshlyn Nicole updated her status.

I actually like who I'm becoming and I can actually say that I love who I am. I'm feeling more confident in myself and embracing the flaws that make me imperfectly perfect.

Dec 14, 2016, 2:58 PM

Thank God Raylan and I are A-okay after this crash! And so is our taxi driver. Thank you to my neighbors that prayed with Raylan and I after this crash. This could have been so much worse. Man, life is so fragile.

Dec 16, 2016, 6:51 PM

Joshlyn Nicole updated her status.

There's so many unrealistic expectations of where you should be in life because everyone is comparing their journeys instead of appreciating their individual journeys.

Jan 5, 2017, 8:11 PM

Joshlyn Nicole updated her status.

I feel motivated to make this world better for my kids, grandkids and great grandkids and so on. But I admit I feel hopeless and I'm not sure how to make this world better. They say it's start with you and you have to be a better human and all of this. Does that change the world or just my world? Idk

Jan 11, 2017, 8:49 AM

Joshlyn Nicole updated her status.

What do I teach my son? Do I teach him to love or hate? Do I teach him to be hopeful or scared? Do I teach him to take the world by storm or teach him to conform to society? I'm teaching him to love, be kind, think outside the box, teaching him to be his own person and to be ready to handle anything. But he will be around kids that are taught the complete opposite.

Jan 11, 2017, 8:53 AM

Current Me
That was pretty much the last post on my old FB account right before I found out I was pregnant with my second child. Reading through all of my posts from high school to my early twenties was an experience. I can see my growth with each post and that was beautiful.

The point of creating this book is to examine my growth and how we evolve as time goes on. There's this new wave that people want to hold you to what you said or did years ago. Sometimes your thoughts are challenged, you begin to see life differently, and your perspective changes.

This was really a fun experience creating this and seeing my many thoughts over the years. I'm much better now and I can honor my progress by seeing how far I've come. Reading through my posts, I realized how miserable I was at times and how much pressure I put on myself.

I really needed this eye-opening experience of staring at my younger self in the mirror. Apologizing to her and forgiving myself. Growth is beautiful and I'm proud of myself.

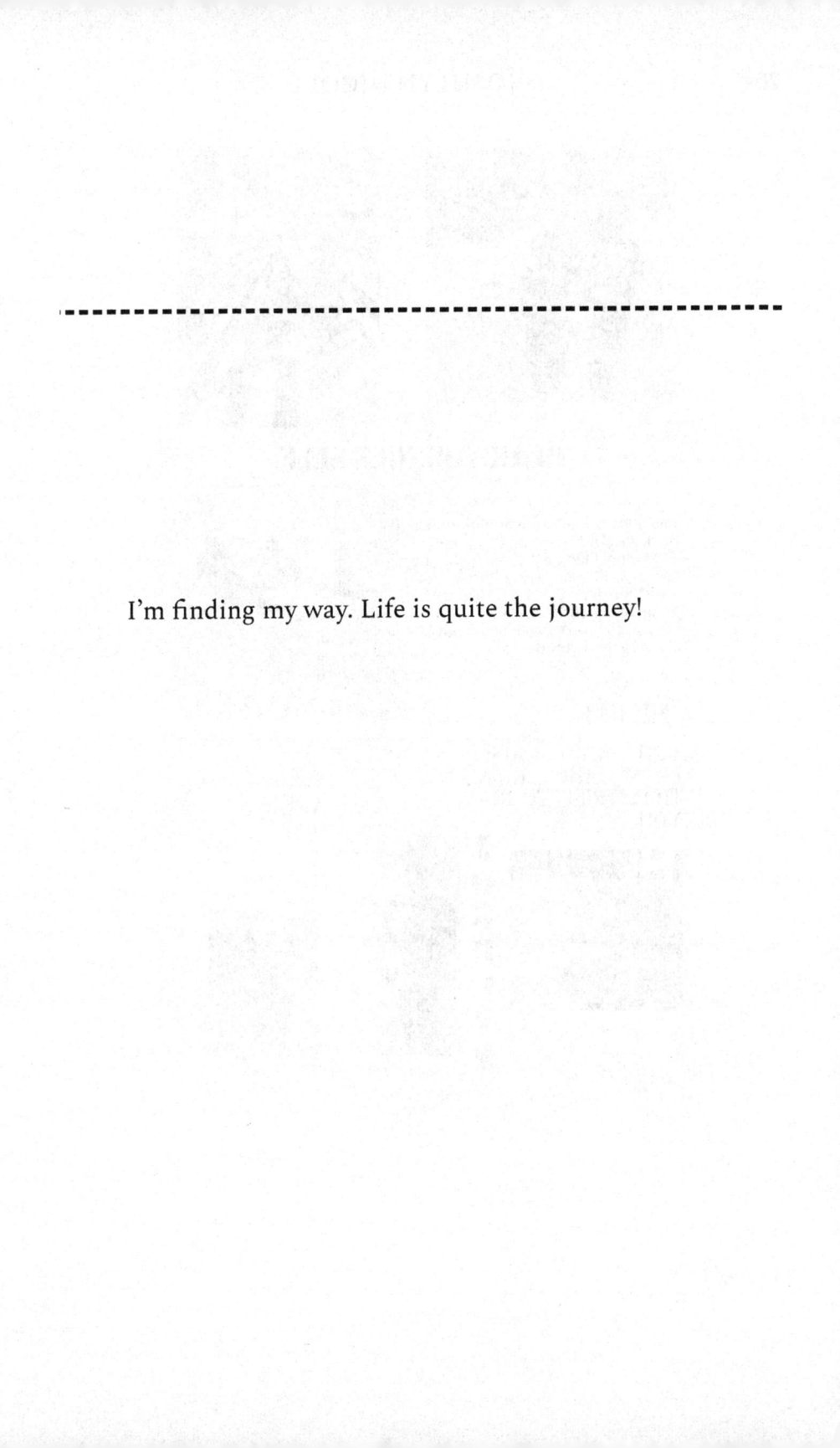

I'm finding my way. Life is quite the journey!

DEAR YOUNGER SELF

You arrived at a beautiful place. Back in 2010, you never imagined life being like this. Even with the last post in 2016, you didn't expect this. Your journey is not meant to be understood by anyone. Keep on your path. You're closer to your dreams than you think.

NICOLE

YOU HAVE RISEN FROM THE RUINS THAT TRIED TO RUIN YOU

YOU ARE NOT A FAILURE

JOSHLYN

Made in the USA
Columbia, SC
25 February 2025